KITCHEN CHAOS

RECIPES FROM A WISCONSIN HOMESTEAD

FIRST EDITION

by Charlie Tennessen

Original watercolor illustrations by Chloé Wright

Cover design by Kristen Cajka

The photos in this book were taken by the author, in and around the four-acre homestead and rented fields.

Additional photos by Chloe Wright (vi, 9, 25, 35, 45, 72) and Everett Soetenga (20, 53)

ISBN: 978-1-7322558-0-7
LCCN: 2018904751

Also from Anarchy Acres:

Rosie's New Harness
Popcorn Day

AnarchyAcres.com/Books

For Mom, who served me the first beans
I ever grew. And for Dad, who chaired
meetings of the Clean Plate Club. That's
how I got here.

Contents

Forward

On one warm summer day the Wisconsin Foodie crew and I were driving through the suburbs, looking for a farm. As we appeared to be getting closer, there was no farm in sight, just row after row of pastel colored homes. Much like a stroll down the aisle of your grocery store, row after row of perfect packaging. What's behind that packaging? What was behind those houses? In our current food culture many of us have no idea what we are eating, how it is made or who is making it. We are attracted to the marketing of a product more than the actual product. With that philosophy in mind, that's the reason we created the television show Wisconsin Foodie. We wanted to help connect people to their food, making it possible for farmers, chefs and food producers to focus on their craft and not worry about advertising. Once you know the story behind a product, you are hooked.

Arriving at the Anarchy Acres address, still no farm, just a typical suburban home. The only difference was a giant combine sitting in the driveway and chickens roaming freely beneath our recently parked car. Once we stepped into the backyard we were immediately transported to a different land and a different time. We now stood on 4 acres of farmland, wheat fields in the distance, goats, donkeys, chickens, produce, and best of all, a freshly lit brick oven. There we met Charlie Tennessen for the first time. Charlie's passion is evident seconds upon meeting him, wide smile and warm handshake. He is part of a new movement of younger farmers who are bringing back unconventional yet once native heritage crops and doing everything by hand (and donkey team). You get the sense that Charlie could be doing a lot of things successfully in his life and career but he has chosen to follow his passion. It is people like Charlie who are making the sacrifices necessary to further our communities and change the mindset of our society through food. He has gone to great lengths to research, find and cultivate forgotten heritage wheats that once blanketed our state.

After a wonderful and engaging day of filming with Charlie, we embarked on a night reminiscent of many in small European towns. The community, friends, animals all packed in the backyard of Anarchy Acres. Dining on freshly baked heritage breads and pizza made from the brick oven and the fields steps away. Now, every time I talk to Charlie, I ask when the next time I can come over to eat his wonderful breads. Luckily for the you, you are holding the holy grail in your hands and can create your own backyard community. The recipes and stories in this book will give you the inspiration to follow your passion while knowing exactly what you are eating.

If we are going to change the world, we have to start one grain at a time. We have to be more conscious of the people around us, the earth beneath us and the foods we consume. We have to be more like Charlie.

–Arthur Ircink, producer of "Wisconsin Foodie" and publisher of *Edible Milwaukee*

Be Your Own Food System

I wrote Kitchen Chaos to inspire people to work with plain ingredients from the farm and garden again. Since moving to my four-acre homestead in 2006, I have deepened a lifelong interest in eating food made with a minimum of processing. I am not a naturally healthy eater. Invite me over to your picnic sometime and you will see me happily munching on potato chips, drinking soda, and eating hot dogs on lily-white buns. But I like being healthy, and I have tried to create a life where I will eat good food as a matter of course.

It's important to me that I know where my food comes from. I prefer food that comes from my farm, food that is nourished by the rain and sun. Off-farm inputs are something I think about often. Of course, I do not use any chemicals or chemical fertilizers, but what else might be coming onto the farm? Did I buy hay from a neighboring farmer? What did my chickens eat? For me, the most beautiful food is that which is created and sustained completely within the confines of my farm. I imagine a high fence on my farm's border, and I consider carefully before allowing anything to breach that barrier.

Foremost is my interest in bread made with heritage grains. I discovered years ago that nearly all bread recipes are tailored for using white flour, or mostly white flour. White flour has been the standard for well over a century. Even current, popular bread recipes that purport to be healthy and traditional often have less than 25% wholemeal flour. It's so confusing for me to read a recipe titled "Whole Wheat Bread" which contains mostly white flour. I've learned that working with freshly milled, whole-grain or nearly whole-grain flour requires different techniques. All the recipes in this book that use flour are tailored towards working with fresh, whole-grain flour.

Today, most people in the West are surrounded by cheap, bountiful food. The food system is efficient, reliable, and pervasive. Unfortunately, the food system does not serve the health or happiness of the people who eat from its table. The food system—the crops, the farmers, the factories, the stores and restaurants—is a thing unto itself. No one controls it, and the food system does not have any goal or mission other than to maintain its existence. In a sense, it's a machine with many moving parts. There are areas of the food system that produce healthy food—healthy for people, and healthy for the rest of creation. Overall, however, the food system is not like this. If you want healthy food, you need to be involved in your own food system.

There is a subtle tyranny to all food systems, from the largest factory down to a single recipe. Once any system is up and running, it tends to exclude inputs that don't fit correctly. A bread factory, for instance, needs all the flour to have an exact protein content. Large chain restaurants need every onion to be the same size. Think of all the foods we never eat because they don't adapt well to our growing and processing systems.

The homesteader is free to use the large onions, and the small ones, and everything in between. Over time, skills in the kitchen increase and possibilities open up for new dishes. Sometimes, you're out of onions (horrors!) and have to find new flavors to work with. Think about your own cooking and the ruts we tend to get into. Keep exploring.

Like a lot of people, I want the food I eat to be beautiful. However, how food looks on the plate is just one small part. The whole cycle is where I find the beauty of food. Who grew the food, where and how it was grown, the type of resources used to create the food, the animals and people who contributed to the food, and what happened to the scraps and waste at the end of a meal. The longer that I live on a farm, where beauty reveals itself effortlessly, the more I think of beauty as a right. All beings deserve to experience beauty. I hope this book inspires you in some small way to seek out and live more a beautiful life.

Ingredients

The heart of any homestead is the cycle of growing, preparing, and eating your own food. There is a conceptual leap from ordinary cooking to homestead cooking. An ordinary cook reads the ingredients listed in a recipe and goes to the store and buys what is needed. A homestead cook looks at the list of ingredients on a recipe, looks at what is available on the homestead that day, and creates a new recipe on the spot. No dish is ever the same twice, since the season and the available ingredients are forever changing. The goal is not to make every dish perfect, but to perfectly utilize what the homestead provides that day. No doubt each homesteader will have different ingredients from what we have on Anarchy Acres.

For me, anyplace where you live and produce food is a homestead. You may produce a small amount of food, or a great deal. What's most important is that you try, that you adapt to the situation, and you learn over time. Each situation, from a city apartment to a 40 acre farm, has an opportunity to produce food. Most important, perhaps, is the interplay of specific crops and varieties with the space and climate limitations that every homesteader deals with. If you live in Alaska, for instance, I'd stay away from growing citrus. If your growing area is small, look for productive foods like corn, beans, or potatoes. Below is the list of ingredients that I grow and cook with most often.

Beans

Beans are either fresh, green-beans, or dried, storage beans. Some people would consider the former a vegetable, and the latter a grain. Either one is fantastic producer in a small plot. Find the varieties that grow best in your region. I have settled on Dragon Tongue as my fresh bean, and Jacob's Cattle for storage.

Fresh beans are easy to freeze. After picking, I cut them in half or sometimes into thirds, and blanch them in boiling water for two minutes. Put portions into a ziploc bag and use a soda straw to suck out as much air as possible. Stack the bags in the freezer.

Dragon Tongue beans ready for the freezer.

Storage beans are also simple. Let them stay on the vine until the pods are brown and wrinkled. Then pick the pods and let them dry further in a covered area. When you have time, crack the pods open and fill up containers with your beans. Save a few for seed and eat the rest over the winter. Last year, an area in the garden ten feet by twenty feet produced 35 pounds of dried beans!

Corn

Flint corn grown on Anarchy Acres.

Corn, like beans, can be divided into grain and vegetable. Corn eaten fresh, or blanched and frozen, is closer to vegetables than it is to grain. But if that same corn develops further and then is dried down, you have a hard grain. A very hard grain, in fact.

The important thing to know about corn is that it absorbs water slowly and is difficult to break down. Corn is so difficult to break down that Native Americans invented the alkali process of nixtamalization to prepare corn and make it more nutritious. New World recipes like tortillas and tamales use nixtamalized corn.

On the homestead, we grow a couple different varieties of sweet corn, flint corn, and popcorn. All are open-pollinated and most are heritage varieties. While corn will not produce as many calories per square foot as beans, it is still a great option for anyone with 500 square feet or more to play with. For sweet corn, we have had our best luck with Bantam Eight-Row and Who Gets Kissed, a modern open-pollinate sweet corn developed at the University of Wisconsin. We also grow and sell a popcorn called Blackjack. Our flint corn is a genetically diverse family of corn called Grand Prairie Flint Composite.

All of the recipes in this book calling for grain corn use flint varieties of corn. The grits, polenta, and corn meal all use the same grind. We mill the cleaned, shelled corn in our stone mill and sift off the heavy pieces with a 700 micron screen.

Potatoes

Potatoes grow well in almost any situation, even containers. On the farm, I like fingerlings the most. Most of the Kenenbecs and Red Norlands I grow are for friends and family. I have not purchased any seed potatoes in recent years. These varieties store well in my root cellar and have been re-planted for years without any disease problems. Like other solanaceous crops, potatoes should be rotated onto new ground as often as space allows.

I have not skinned a potato in decades. Potato skins have a greater concentration of vitamins and fiber than the rest of the potato, and they taste great. I recommend a generous scrubbing and no peeling for any potato in your kitchen.

Squash

This is one area where I don't mess around with exotic varieties much. The butternut squash works just great for us on Anarchy Acres. It's easy to grow, stores well, and tastes great. Every year I grab the seeds out of the last good squash in the root cellar and plant them for the following season.

If you don't have a root cellar, one easy alternative is to dice and freeze after harvest. To do this, just cut a squash in half and remove all the seeds. (If you're ambitious, you can toast the seeds and eat them.) Now slice off all the skin and discard. Once you are down to all-orange flesh, cut everything up into cubes around ¾ inch square. These cubes can be bagged and frozen, and used any time over the next couple of years.

Wheat and Wheat Flour

Flour is a food shaped by the machines and methods which handle wheat. Since mechanization, both wheat and flour have changed to suit the interests of the "wheat machine." First, wheat is moved into the field and planted, by machines. Later, mature wheat is harvested, dried, milled, and sifted. Although wheat and wheat flour have fed people for at least 8,000 years, the food machines of the last two centuries have done more to change wheat than in all of the previous 7,800 years of wheat cultivation.

Foremost among the changes that wheat has undergone is the development of white flour, which today is almost ubiquitous. White flour was developed as a matter of fashion first, and subsequently as a way to extend the shelf life of flour. White flour became widespread in the mid-19th century, when cost-efficient sifting machines were invented. When flour is intensively sifted, using a screen of 200 microns or less, it can be stored almost indefinitely without attracting insects. Unfortunately for people who eat products made with white flour, however, small-screen sifting removes all of the fiber, and nearly all

of the vitamins and minerals, from the flour. In fact, at the time white flour became common, people who ate bread as a staple food often developed the wasting disease beriberi, because their bread no longer contained any vitamins.

At the same time that intensive flour sifting became common, harvesting machines were being invented and sold to farmers. These machines work better with wheat varieties that have less genetic variability than previous generations of wheat. Eventually, most bread was produced in factories, which again require a very uniform raw material (flour) to perform well. Also, white flour dough rises faster and spends less time in the bread factory. Less time equals more loaves per day, which equals more profit. All of these factors have combined to make modern wheat and flour different from what people used before the mid-19th Century. The recipes in this book are tailored for older wheat and flour.

The flour we eat at Anarchy Acres is from heritage variety wheat, ground fresh on our stone mill. We use a large sifting screen to pull of the largest pieces of bran that escape the stones, which we then feed to the chickens and goats. This flour is different from white flour and the whole wheat flour purchased in most supermarkets. I personally find any store-bought flour to taste stale. I have never found any flour from other producers that has the same fresh, floral fragrance that our flour has. I encourage anyone with an interest in health and good flavor to purchase a home mill and start making their own flour at home.

Eggs

I have always had a small flock of chickens on the farm. Anarchy Acres is located in a special place, and in general we have relatively low pressure from predators. This means that the chickens go outside every day and roam over most of the farm, and several adjacent properties as well. The neighbors don't mind, although I occasionally get a concerned phone call that goes something like, "Your chickens are in my backyard—help!" Chickens come home to roost, fortunately, so there is not much to worry about. While they are not roosting, the "girls" are out scratching in the dirt, or digging in the compost pile, and just generally getting exercise and a widely variable diet.

It's exciting to me that the chickens get all their food from the farm, and that a mere dozen chickens have access to well over 10 acres of space to roam. Most backyard chickens live off feed purchased from the store—a regrettable off-farm input. I'm able to feed my chickens excess wheat, which they do well on. During the summer, when there are so many worms and insects to feed on, the flock eats very little wheat feed while actually increasing their egg output. And the egg quality is fantastic!

Summer Vegetables

I grow the "usual suspects" of annual vegetables on the farm. Tomatoes, carrots, kale, chard, lettuce, turnips, brussel sprouts, etc. As a general rule I don't mess around too much with things that take a lot of babysitting. Except for a drip line that I set up for tomatoes and peppers, I do not irrigate my quarter-acre garden. I expect my plants to set deep roots and to take care of themselves. Most of the lettuce I grow is eaten on-the-spot while weeding or otherwise working in the garden. I direct-seed most of the plants, timing the planting to coincide with wet or cloudy weather while the seeds are germinating. I find I learn more about plants, and about being a good farmer, by this "hands off" approach. Of course, other people are in different situations.

Alliums

Recipes that don't start off with "first, fry an onion" are immediately suspect in my way of thinking. Onions, shallots, scallions, and garlic are primary components of a well-lived life. I grow a couple different standard varieties of onions every year, like Ailsa Craig. My garlic is a hard-neck variety I've had for years, whose origin is lost to me. It's vaguely purple, tastes great, and keeps until the scapes appear in June. My garlic produces big bulbs which are easy to peel. I love the taste of shallots but I find them a pain to deal with in the kitchen, due to their small size. I have not grown shallots in recent years. Spring onions are

lovely but I don't plant onions specifically for this purpose. Most of the spring onions I consume are thinnings or volunteers that I find in the garden. I'll bet that I eat some kind of allium from the farm every day.

Herbs and Spices

On the farm, we put spices in everything! Basil, oregano, rosemary, thyme, hot peppers, and others. Many herbs can be used fresh, and later dried. Basil during the summer can be eaten whole in salads, or chopped and put onto a pizza. For the off-season, I pick leaves and let them dry in a basket. Oregano goes through the same life cycle.

Hot peppers, also, can be used either fresh or dried. Small peppers like serranos and jalapenos can be dried by hanging on a string. Larger peppers like aleppos will usually spoil if you don't give them some help while drying out. I usually put my aleppos in the oven, set as low as it will go, for a few hours. Then they can be crushed and used as needed throughout the winter.

I adore fresh parsley, but it's not always around when you need some. The plants can go to seed quickly in summer heat. I have had good luck blanching and freezing parsley. To get it in the freezer, wash the parsley and chop it up a little. Blanch in boiling water for one minute, remove, and drain as best you can. Get it into ziploc bags in thin layers, and use a soda straw to suck out the air. Although frozen parsley is not going to work great as a garnish anymore, it will still work very well for salsa. I feel that salsa is just not right without parsley, so I try to keep some in the freezer.

Honey and Maple Syrup

I keep one or two bee colonies out next to the garden, although I don't claim to be a great beekeeper. The past few seasons they have tended to die over the winter, so I start out with fresh colonies most every spring. However, the bees always find good nectar and every year I extract at least 75 pounds of honey. I sell the surplus and use the rest in cookies, pancakes, muffins, and iced tea.

I also make one to two gallons of maple syrup every spring. Although the farm does not have any mature sugar maple trees, the ash-leaf maples (also called box elders) that grow along the fence lines make great syrup. Boiling sap is a great activity for March when there's nothing really to do, but you're dying to get outside and do something.

Off-farm Inputs

A person can't do everything, although I do believe that striving for self-sufficiency is a legitimate life philosophy. On Anarchy Acres, the primary off-farm inputs to the kitchen are butter, sugar (for those cursed cookies I'm hooked on), vanilla, oil, salt, black pepper, and meat. And energy.

The elephant in everyone's room is energy. The food that an average American eats every year uses up the equivalent of 400-500 gallons of gasoline. About two thirds of this sum is consumed as agricultural chemicals—fertilizers, pesticides, herbicides, and fungicides. Energy, usually oil, is the driver. In one sense, we are eating oil.

Since agricultural has been around for 10,000 years, but massive energy sources like petroleum and coal have only been used for the past couple of centuries, I am concerned about the sustainability of the present system. I doubt highly that the current food system will survive another 10,000 years in its present form. On Anarchy Acres, I do as much as I can to reduce the energy my food takes to produce.

The biggest step I've taken towards energy independence is to use a team of miniature donkeys to till my garden and do the heavy lifting on the farm. Rosie, Cassie, and Sebastian—Team Anarchy—are my regular companions on the farm. I have resolved that no tractor will be used on my homestead fields, just animal power. The donkeys and I work and play together, and we even come close to sharing the same food. In summer, for instance, when I eat corn on the cob, the spent cobs get tossed to the donkeys, who eagerly consume them. This cycle is the whole point of animal-powered agriculture. A donkey or similar draft animal can eat grass that is grown on the farm, and use that plant energy to pull a plow. The farm, receiving only sunshine and rain, grows the food that powers the draft team. The donkeys even grow themselves. Their young foals can take over the work for the team when they get old.

Do I get all my food off the farm? No. If it's been a long day, I drive into town and eat from the taco truck. I'm the weirdo who shows up with his own plate, since I don't want them to waste a styrofoam plate on my order. Chorizo tacos with rice and beans go a long way towards healing a tired farmer, and I don't consider it cheating.

Breakfast

Mornings on the farm vary by the season. In high summer, farmers rise early to get their work done before heat and insects make work outside unbearable. In winter, farmers hibernate and take more time in beginning the work day. Summer offers a bounty of fresh ingredients and eggs. In winter, veggies are coming out of the root cellar or the freezer, and the chickens are often on strike (no eggs). Here are the main ways I deal with the first meal of the day on Anarchy Acres.

Three Grain Sourdough Pancakes

I can't function without pancakes during the winter months. Here is my reason for getting out of bed on a sub-zero Saturday morning.

Makes about 21 four-inch pancakes

Corn meal	½ cup
Buckwheat flour	½ cup
Wheat flour	½ cup
Sourdough starter (optional)	½ cup
Honey (or molasses, or sugar, or something else)	3 tablespoons
Salt	½ teaspoon
Baking soda	1 teaspoon
Vegetable oil or melted butter	3 tablespoons
Egg	1
Milk, (any kind)	2 cups

The grain ingredients for pancakes are fungible—it can be all wheat flour, 50/50 wheat flour and buckwheat flour, or different combinations of wheat flour, corn meal, and buckwheat flour. Just make the dry ingredients add up to 1 ½ cups or so. I would limit the corn meal to 1/3 of the total grains. I always add sourdough starter. This makes for a smoother taste, and it helps keep my starter strong. But sourdough starter is not necessary if you don't have some. As always with pancakes, you will be adjusting the final consistency. Whole grains, especially corn, take a long time to hydrate. I often make the batter the night before, which results in a smoother, more savory pancake. I have good luck keeping it in the fridge when there is some left over, for two or three days. Enjoy!

Corn Muffins

Although I can eat corn muffins any time of the day, breakfast is the most natural time to eat them. I rarely bake them in the morning, however. Usually I make a couple of batches and store them in the freezer. When reheated correctly, they can actually taste better out of the freezer.

To reheat muffins, place the muffin directly onto the rack of an oven at 375 degrees. Pull them out if you see any sign of browning. Usually 12-14 minutes is about right. Most mornings I can put one in the oven, go feed the animals, and get back inside just in time to eat a warm corn muffin made from grains I grow myself.

Makes 11 muffins when using a cast-iron muffin pan

Corn meal	1 cup
Wheat flour	1 cup
Honey (or molasses, or sugar, or something else)	¼ cup
Salt	½ teaspoon
Baking powder	2 teaspoons
Vegetable oil or melted butter	¼ cup
Egg	1
Milk, (any kind)	1 cup

Preheat oven to 400 degrees. I use a cast iron muffin pan which I preheat a bit to make greasing it with butter easier. But grease it with something. You can also use an 8-inch or 9-inch square or round pan.

Beat everything together with a wooden spoon, it should be about like pancake batter (not too thick or the muffins may taste dry). Remember, whole grains and all the accompanying bran will soak up a lot of moisture and oil. Too little liquid will result in a dry product.

Bake for 20-25 minutes in your 400 degree oven. After removing from the oven, I let them sit in the cast-iron pan for 10-15 minutes. This let's the muffins shrink a bit, and then they can be tipped out with a dull knife very easily. I let them finish cooling on a rack if I'm going to freeze them. Otherwise they can be eaten immediately.

Batter going into the 11-hole Griswold No. 10 cast-iron muffin pan.

Grits

Grits are what you get when you make oatmeal out of cornmeal. I don't grow oats, so if I want hot cereal I eat grits. If you want to sound fancy, you can call grits polenta. But polenta and grits are really the same thing.

On the farm, I mill all my corn in a single pass through the stone mill and run it through a 700 micron screen. I put the stones close together to get as much to pass through the screen as possible. Whatever comes through the screen is used for grits and all my other recipes that call for corn meal. The little bit that gets sifted out (less than 5%) goes to my chickens. In the marketplace, ground corn is usually graded into corn flour, corn meal, and grits, according to the coarseness of the grind. I prefer to use a "one-size-fits-all" approach. I like to mill just enough to last a month or two. I notice the loss of freshness after just a couple of weeks.

Serves two people

Corn meal	½ cup
Water	1 ¾ cup
Salt	¼ teaspoon

I prefer to make grits using an overnight cold soak. Mix everything together the night before in your favorite saucepan. Let it sit on the stove, and first thing in the morning, turn the burner on low. Now you can go do your chores while your grits heat up. Stir a couple of times if you are able. The grits can be eaten in about 25 minutes. If you did not soak overnight, simmer for about 50 minutes, stirring regularly.

There are two schools of thought regarding condiments for grits: savory, or sweet. If you like savory, find a decent hot sauce and put as much on as you like. I prefer sweet, so I put a pad of butter on and then drizzle maple syrup from the farm on top. The above ratio will make a somewhat firm texture, which is how I like it. If you prefer your hot cereal to be more runny, add a little more water. How well your cover seals will also affect the final texture, since water may boil off during cooking.

Grits topped with butter and maple syrup, ready for the farmer.

Scrambler

Unless my chickens are on strike, which happens from time to time, I have two eggs most mornings. If the morning schedule allows, I like to have my carbs first (toast, grits, or muffins) and then run out and do chores and maybe some work in the garden. I then have eggs in the mid-morning, which I sometimes call second breakfast.

I never eat scrambled eggs without putting something in. In summertime, I inspect the garden soon after dawn and grab a few leaves of whatever is available. This could be spinach, swiss chard, kale, or bok choi. I always add an allium of some sort, too. A spring onion, garlic, garlic scapes, or an onion sitting in the root cellar will do. I like to get as much flavor and fiber into scrambled eggs as I can.

Summertime Scrambler—serves one

Eggs	2 or 3
Oil	1 tablespoon
Allium (onion, scallion, garlic, etc), chopped	variable
Kale, chard, spinach, or pepper, chopped	variable
Salt and pepper	to taste

Take your smoke alarm off the wall and get a cast-iron frying pan good and hot on the stove. If you're having toast, press the toaster down now. Add the oil and chopped allium first. The green ingredients or pepper can be added 30 seconds later. Scramble the eggs in a bowl, remembering to add black pepper and salt at the same time. Dump the contents into the hot frying pan. Keep stirring. If it takes longer than than a minute to cook the eggs, try getting the frying pan hotter next time. Get the eggs and toast onto a plate ASAP, grab your tea or coffee, and eat!

When you're done, put the smoke alarm on the wall, go back outside, and get to work.

Frying up some onions and peppers prior to adding the eggs.

Schtick Bread

Schtick bread is any bread fried in bacon grease. The recipe comes from deep in my childhood, and I'm hardly even sure the spelling is correct. Family lore says that my great grandmother ate schtick bread every day of her life. Although this woman lived well into her 90s, I was too young to know her before she died. Growing up in the anti-fat 1970s, we only ate schtick bread sparingly, and only from my Dad. By the time I went to high school, the family's thinking was that schtick bread very unhealthy and should be avoided.

Now that I live on a homestead, and I try to conserve as much as I can, I see schtick bread a little differently. I wonder about the ethics of eating bacon but throwing away the grease. This seems a little unfair to the pig, adding insult to injury after deciding to eat the pig in the first place. Furthermore, nutritional thinking about fat has changed since I grew up. Fat is not the bogeyman as much anymore, and now I can eat my schtick bread a little more openly.

When I eat bacon, I'll save the grease and toast pieces of my bread in the frying pan until the grease is gone. The recipe couldn't be simpler.

Get the grease good and hot. If you're already frying the bacon, that's how hot the skillet should be. If the bread is coming out of the freezer, thaw it out first. The oil should dance a little when you drop the bread in. If everything is right, the bread should turn golden brown after little more than 30 seconds. Turn once, season with salt and pepper, and eat!

Lunch

"Lunch" is a pretty loose term on the farm. If the crops and the weather are lining up, the work keeps going and lunch gets pushed aside. In quieter times, especially in winter, lunch might end up being the main meal of the day. Here are some things that I see on the lunch table pretty regularly.

Summer Stir Fry

If time permits, lunch in the summertime often consists of fresh greens, steamed in a frying pan, seasoned with soy sauce and apple cider vinegar. Here's what I mean.

Summer stir fry—serves 1, with leftovers

Eggs	optional
Oil	1-2 tablespoons
Allium (onion, scallion, garlic, etc), chopped	½ cup
Kale, chard, spinach, or pepper, chopped	4 cups, or more
Soy sauce	2 tablespoons
Apple cider vinegar	2 tablespoons

If you are going to add egg, cook that first. Heat up your skillet, add a little oil, and brown a bit of onion or garlic. Then crack in as many eggs as you plan to use, scramble with the spatula, and set it aside once it's cooked.

Fry up the rest of the onion, and once it has started to brown you can add the carrots, stems, broccoli, or whatever takes the longest to cook. If you're including minced garlic or garlic scapes, that goes in, too. Sprinkle in a bit of soy sauce and apple cider vinegar, or water. Cover for a minute to get it steamy in there. Once the stems and carrots are at least half-cooked, add the leafy greens and more liquid if needed. Keep stirring and use the cover as needed. If you made egg, stir it back in towards the end. The stir fry is ready once the leaves are wilting.

Tortillas

If you live in the New World, you should make tortillas at some point. It's possibly the most historically significant food on the two continents. You will be nixtamalizing the corn, a process that uses alkali to release additional nutrients locked in the germ.

Makes 20-25 tortillas

Flint corn, dent corn, or flour corn	1 pound
Lime cal	2 tablespoons
Water	2 quarts

First, nixtamalize the corn and make the masa dough. Find a stainless steel pot and lid that you don't care about too much. The limewater will tend to stain the pot. Don't use aluminum—it's too reactive. Rinse the corn, cover with at least an inch of water, and mix in the lime cal. You can get lime cal in small packages at a Mexican grocery, or purchase it by the sack in a brickyard. (Lime cal is also used to make cement.) Alternatively, you can use fresh ash from a hardwood fire. Use about 2 cups of sifted ash in place of the cal.

Bring to a boil and let simmer for 75 minutes, making sure the corn stays covered with water. The corn absorbs a lot of water, so keep an eye on it. Put the cover on and let it sit overnight.

Rinsing the pericarp off the corn after the overnight soak in alkali.

When you are ready to press the dough and cook the tortillas, the corn first needs to be rinsed and rubbed. The outer covering (pericarp) of the corn kernels should have loosened up by now. Pour off the lime water, rinse well, and use your fingers to get most of the pericarp off. Keep rinsing. The cleaned kernels are called hominy, and they can be used as-is in soups and other recipes. However, we are going to turn our hominy into masa dough.

Cast-iron corn grinders are easily available online for less than $100. Clamp or bolt it down to something sturdy—it takes moderate effort to mill the nixtamalized corn. Set the milling plates as close together as possible, and grind up the corn. It will take about five minutes of continuous cranking to mill the amount of corn in this recipe.

Hydrate the dough before pressing the tortillas, using ½ cup or more of water. Mix it up with your hands and get the consistency even.

Milling masa dough with the hand cranked counter top corn grinder.

Press and cook the tortillas. Press enough dough in your hand to make a ball the size of a golf ball. Using a press covered with waxed paper, crush the ball into a thin tortilla. Cook the tortillas in a hot frying pan, using little or no oil. The hotter, the better. You may want to take the smoke alarm off the wall again. Ideally, the tortillas will bubble a bit as they cook. Turn the tortilla after 45 seconds or so.

Fresh-pressed tortilla ready for cooking.

Although masa dough can be stored in the refrigerator, I find the hydration and texture is never the same as it is when the dough is fresh. So I use all the dough up immediately and put extra tortillas in the refrigerator.

Tortillas can be eaten by themselves, or wrapped around some beans to make a taco. By cutting up and frying or baking them, you'll have tortilla chips. Either way, the flavor of tortillas from home-grown and home-processed corn is impressive.

Homestead Tacos

So now that you have a pile of tortillas, you can have tacos for lunch all week long! Here's what I do.

Tacos For One

Tortillas	2-3
Chopped onion	½ cup
Oil	1 tablespoon
Cilantro, chopped (if you've got some)	¼ cup
Cooked beans	½ cup
Chorizo sausage or ground meat	optional
Salsa or hot sauce	yes

Heat up a cast-iron frying pan, add the oil, and add the onion. You may want to reserve a little of the onion to have some to top the finished taco. Once the onion has started to brown, add any meat that you are going to use. After the meat has browned, put in the beans.

Simultaneously, you can run a second frying pan to heat up the tortillas if they have been in the fridge. Place the contents of the first frying pan into 2 or 3 tortillas, sprinkle on onion and cilantro, top with salsa or hot sauce, and enjoy. You're eating a perfectly balanced meal that came almost entirely from your garden.

Don't despair if your homemade corn tortillas break or tear. The flavor and nutrition will still be fantastic. To improve your tortillas, make sure the masa dough is well hydrated and properly nixtamalized. The corn grinder should be set to grind as finely as possible. Finally, cooking tortillas on a super-hot griddle goes a long way to ensuring a strong tortilla.

Tabbouleh

This savory and satisfying side dish showcases heritage wheat berries. A few high-quality ingredients allow this simple but tasty version of tabbouleh to shine.

Makes 4 servings

Uncooked wheat berries	3/4 cup
Water	1 ½ cups
Parsley, chopped	1-2 bunches
Celery, diced	2 ribs
Chopped tomato	optional
Chopped, fresh mint	optional
Olive oil	2 tablespoons
Lemon juice	1 lemon
Salt and pepper	to taste
Ground cumin	pinch (optional)

Combine uncooked wheat berries with water and a pinch of salt in a medium saucepan. Cover, bring to a boil and let simmer about 1 hour or until wheat berries are tender but slightly chewy. Wheat berries will yield about 1 ½ cups once cooked. Drain off any excess water. Cool to room temperature. Toss cooled wheat berries with remaining ingredients in a large bowl. If time allows, let tabbouleh sit in the refrigerator to slightly chill and absorb the flavors.

Summer Salad

I don't make many salads on the farm, so I'm not going to share a recipe. Most of the lettuce I eat is a bite here and there while I weed the garden. I call it my "cave man" salad, just grabbing tasty leaves that catch my eye. But to me, lettuce is not the essence of homesteading. If you grow greens and a few tomatoes, there is still the problem of where your food comes from. A cup of lettuce has five calories, which is less energy than it takes me to walk out to my garden. There are no world civilizations founded on eating greens, because the total nutritional impact of a green salad is pretty low. Salad is nice, but it does not sustain life.

On the other hand, we have all sorts of civilizations throughout history that have been fed by corn, wheat, rye, beans, and even potatoes. This is one reason why I've been drawn to these foods. They pack a punch, and if I cultivate them, I have the possibility of getting significant, life-giving calories off of my small patch of earth.

Anyhow, don't let me stop you from eating a good salad! And if you do make a salad, consider adding some cooked wheat berries on top. They have a wonderful chewy texture, taste great, and will add more nutrition to your salad. Use the first part of the tabbouleh recipe on page 32 to cook the wheat berries.

Winter Vegetables

The lowly frozen vegetable is a great way to extend the taste of summer into the off-season. From July to September, I am busy stocking away green beans and sweet corn, to provide sustenance and vitamins year-round.

I grow dragon tongue beans for freezing. They are washed, cut, and blanched for about 2 minutes in boiling water. Then I put them in a ziploc bag and suck out the air with a soda straw. Sweet corn needs to blanch a little longer—you'll see the color get a little deeper and richer when it's ready. There are devices to help cut corn off the cob, or you can cut it off with any sharp knife. Every time I eat sweet corn during the harvest season, I end up freezing a little bit. Whether I boil the corn or roast it on an outdoor grill, I just cook as much as I can, eat what I eat, and freeze the rest. By September the freezer downstairs is bursting.

My main sweet corn the last two years has been an open-pollinated variety developed at the University of Wisconsin called "Who Gets Kissed." I love that it comes from my alma mater, that I can save my own seed, and that it tastes great!

When I'm hungry I go into the freezer and break off frozen chunks of beans and corn. If you froze them in thin layers, this is easy to do. I always mix beans with corn. Get your favorite saucepan, put the corn and beans in, and drizzle a little olive oil on top. Put in salt and pepper, plus a tablespoon or two of water. Cover the lid and cook on high. Frozen vegetables will have the best texture if you cook them quickly.

Dinner

Even if I've had a big lunch and won't be eating too much, I still have more time around dinner and tend to make the larger dishes at this time. It's almost a given that dinner will involve making extra, so I have leftovers for the next few days. It's also what I think about and plan out all day long. Once I'm happy with a dinner recipe, I invite over a few friends for feedback and socialization. I hope you can do the same with some of these dinner dishes.

Soup from a Farm

Basic soup ingredients

Medium onion, chopped	1
Garlic cloves	3-6 cloves
Olive oil	1 tablespoon
Salt	½ teaspoon
Black pepper	yes
Potatoes	3 large, or equivalent amount
Turnips	optional
Carrots	optional
Kale, chopped	optional
Stock or water	3-4 cups to start with

Soup from a farm—fancy that! Just like "Stone Soup," homestead soup can have all kinds of ingredients. The above list is just a starting point. Leeks, broccoli, kholarabi, bok choi, parsnips are just a few more options that come to mind. Each soup you make will be unique.

Begin by frying the onion in oil. You could also use a leek or some shallots. Don't be afraid to brown them—that will add good flavor. While the onions are frying, chop the potatoes into inch-thick cubes. Add the potatoes once the onions have started to brown, and fry the potatoes a bit.

I do not peel potatoes or other root vegetables. I simply scrub them in cold water with a stiff brush. Most kale leaves have a bitter stem that is best discarded before chopping up the leaf. I sometimes peel a turnip if it's unusually large and woody. However, when turnips get too big I usually just feed them to the animals.

Once the onions start to caramelize, add the stock or water. Put in the salt and pepper, and as much garlic as you like. Keep in mind that store-bought soup stock can have a lot of salt in it, so compensate accordingly.

I'm a garlic addict, so I use around six cloves. The garlic can be crushed or minced. If you're going to include turnips, they should also be diced and added at this time.

Simmer for about 15 minutes, stirring occasionally. Now take a potato masher and crush all the potatoes. This will dramatically thicken the soup, and it's the reason you can make this soup without stock.

After crushing the potatoes, add carrots or other ingredients that you don't want to be crushed. The chopped kale also goes in at this time, too. Resume simmering. If you want to add dumplings, use the instructions below.

Heritage flour dumplings (optional)

Flour	1 cup
Salt	¼ teaspoon
Water	⅓ cup

Dumplings work the same way that pasta or noodles do in soup. I use the simplest possible dumpling recipe, and it works great. Stir the flour and salt with a wooden spoon, then mix in the water until you have a sticky dough. Use a tablespoon and drop dumpling-sized bits of the dough into the soup until the dough is used up. Stir gently until the dumplings start to cook and firm up.

Simmer the soup another 20 minutes, and serve. Add water to get the consistency you like. Most soup I make tastes better the second day. I just keep putting the whole pot back into the refrigerator when it's cool, and then re-heating on the stove for the next meal.

Basic Beans

If you're going to be living on a sustainable, home-grown diet in North America, it's probably going to involve beans. Beans are beautiful, delicious, healthy, and nutritious. Growing and eating your own beans is the most significant step most people can take towards improving the outlook for our environment. Here's how we prepare beans in the Anarchy Acres kitchen.

Beans—enough for a week of meals

Dried beans	1 pound
Oil	1-2 tablespoons
Allium (onion, scallion, garlic, etc), finely chopped	1 cup
Diced tomatoes	2 cups
Water	5 cups total, including the tomatoes
Salt	½ teaspoon, at least
Pepper flakes, bay leaves, black pepper, oregano	yes

I have always cooked beans in a pressure cooker. Although I began with an ordinary stove-top pressure cooker, in recent years I have used an electric pressure cooker with a timer. This unit automatically switches to a "keep warm" mode after cooking, which is fantastic. The beans can stay on that setting for hours just fine.

Begin with the cooker on the saute or browning setting, and get the oil and onions going. In the meantime, measure and rinse out the beans. Two cups of beans equals about 1 pound for most varieties.

When the onion has been browned, dump in the beans and liquid. I count the tomatoes as liquid, so just put your diced tomatoes into a glass measure and add water up to the line. I always have frozen tomatoes in the freezer. Just cut your tomatoes into large chunks, place in a ziploc, suck the air out with a straw, and freeze.

Put any spice you can think of in there before closing the lid. I crush in at least 6 garlic cloves, and usually add oregano, basil, or bay leaves. Definitely add some black pepper, and some kind of hot pepper, too. You can put in hot pepper flakes or an entire dried chipotle pepper. After cooking, remove the chipotle,

Jacob's Cattle beans and miscellaneous, frozen tomatoes waiting for the pressure cooker.

mince it, and put as much back into the beans as you want. If you're lazy, or in a hurry, any kind of seasoned salt will help. I find the Goya Adobo "All Purpose Seasoning" works great.

Secure the cover and cook on the high setting for around 75 minutes. If you're using the stove-top style of pressure cooker, the pressure release should be moderately dancing. Beans usually taste better the second day. You can even use the pressure cooker with the lid on to speed up the reheating, and to soften the beans if the first cooking was not enough. I like some bean texture leftover in the dish, but if you are going for pure bean paste just keep cooking them.

Beans taste great over a bed of brown rice, but since I don't grow rice I rarely do this. Beans can be eaten as-is after cooking, wrapped into a tortilla, or used as corn-chip dip. Regardless of how I eat them, I usually add my favorite hot sauce or salsa.

Pasta

If you want to impress, make fresh pasta at home! It's easy to make, and it's healthy and great tasting when you start with fresh, stone-ground flour.

Serves 2-3 people

Flour	1 ⅓ cups
Eggs	2
Salt and pepper	pinch
Herbs and spices	optional
Olive oil	½ teaspoon

Pasta dough can be made up quickly and easily using an ordinary food processor. The key is to get the hydration right on the first try. Crack the eggs into the food processor, add the

olive oil and spices, and pulse a couple times to scramble the eggs. Add the flour, and now run the food processor continuously. If everything is right, the dough will first form crumbles and then come together into a single, stiff ball in 30 seconds or less. If the ball does not form, check the consistency. If it's too wet, add some flour, and if it's too dry, add a little water. When you get it right, the ball will be sticky but firm.

Now it's time to roll out the noodles and have some fun. The key to rolling pasta is to roll it multiple times, putting the rollers closer together each time through. If the dough sticks to the rollers, mix in some more flour. If the ribbon comes out crumbly, fold it together and run it through again, several times if necessary. Keep the portions small. As soon as the ribbon is longer than 2 feet, cut it in half. The pieces can be staged on a counter dusted with flour. Roll it a little thinner on each pass. On my machine, I roll down to the "5" setting, on a scale of 1-9.

If you want to save pasta to cook another day, you have two possibilities. The traditional method is to dry the pasta. Just drape it over a wooden dowel, or a laundry drying rack. After an overnight drying you can store the pasta in bags or rigid containers. Another possibility is to keep the pasta hydrated and use refrigeration. To do this, dust the pasta with flour to prevent sticking, and put in a covered container in the refrigerator. It will last a couple of weeks this way.

Most of the time, however, I roll and boil at the same time. I like to have the water already boiling when I start rolling. For an 8 quart pot, drop ⅛ cup of salt in with the boiling water. When it's time to run the ribbons through the cutter, I go directly from the cutter to the hot water.

Homemade whole wheat pasta topped with fresh-grated Parmesan is a meal unto itself. On the farm, I usually top with Parmesan plus a dollop of basil pesto. It's heavenly.

Roasted Root Vegetables

Just as I said about beans, if you're going to live off the land in North America, it's going to involve some root vegetables. Potatoes, carrots, turnips, beets, and onions. For our purposes here, we'll count squash as a root vegetable, too. These are the foods that will be coming out of the homestead root cellar in January. I'll give you two strategies for roasting vegetables for winter time meals.

First Strategy: Marinate and Bake. This strategy works best when the vegetables involved all have approximately the same cooking time. Potatoes, carrots, and onion will all finish cooking at the same time if the preparation is correct. Dice up the carrots and potatoes. The onions should be sliced into wedges. Put everything into a glass baking container and add oil, herbs, black pepper, and salt. Toss it all together and put in the oven at 475 degrees. If you don't have a glass baking container, you can put everything onto an ordinary cookie sheet. Stir vegetables once or twice, and start checking them after 30 minutes. They should for sure be done after 40 minutes.

Alternate Strategy: Boil, fry, and bake. This is the strategy I use when I have ingredients with widely varying cook times. Listed in order from longest to shortest cooking time, the vegetables I eat a lot of are: Beets, Turnips, Potatoes, Carrots, Onions, and Squash. To make a fantastic roasted dish with these ingredients, begin with a basic cleanup in the sink. Turnips and beets do not need to be peeled—just cut off the root and the top, and scrub well with a brush. The same goes for the carrots and potatoes. Butternut squash gets peeled with a knife. Cut the squash in half and start taking off slices of the skin in long peels. Go deep enough to get past the white stuff so it's all beautiful orange color. Slice through the hollow part and dig out all the seeds. I rinse the seeds off and put them on a towel to dry. A few choice seeds will be planted next year, and the remainder roasted and eaten.

Once the ingredients are cleaned up you can begin chopping and dicing. The turnips, beets, and potatoes will be boiled. Beets take the longest, around 30 minutes. Turnips will take less, and most potatoes can be boiled in 10 minutes. If you're using one pot, just put the beets in first, then the turnips, and finally the potatoes. Use a cooking fork with thin tines to poke them occasionally and monitor the cooking. You should be able to slide a fork in easily. You can also use the size of each piece as a strategy to synchronize the cook time. Make the potatoes the largest pieces, and the beets the smallest.

While things are boiling, start frying the onion. After a minute or two you can add the diced squash. If you can brown the squash a bit the flavor will be heavenly! The boiled vegetables, drained, can be added at this time. Add your salt and spices and fry for a few more minutes. Then put the frying pan in a 375 degree oven for 20 minutes. Take care removing the hot pan from the oven, and you're ready to eat. This dish makes outstanding leftovers, so don't worry if there is too much. They are delicious, cold or reheated.

We're ready to eat, folks!

Tamales

This traditional Mexican dish originated in Mesoamerica somewhere between 5,000 and 8,000 years ago. You can't get much more authentic than this! Tamales are also very adaptable and not that difficult to make.

Makes Around 20 Tamales

Fresh masa dough	1 pound dry corn
Onion, chopped	1 cup
Oil	1-2 tablespoons
Dried corn husks	20
Garlic	if you like
Hot peppers, minced	to taste
Cooked beans	1 ½ cups
Sausage or ground meat	optional
Favorite salsa or hot sauce	enough

Prepare masa dough as described in the tortilla recipe on page 29. Soak your corn husks in warm water while you prepare the tamale filling. The corn husks can be saved from your harvest or purchased at a Mexican grocery store. It helps if they can soak for a few hours.

The filling can be all kinds of things—meat, cheese, fruit, or vegetables. Technically, you can put anything edible inside there and it will still be a tamale. For this recipe, however, we're going to use beans grown on the farm. The result will be a healthy, balanced, and complete food source made entirely of New World crops grown on the homestead.

Heat up your skillet, put the oil in, and start frying the onion. If you're going to use meat, chop it up and add now. Minced garlic can also be added at this time. Once the onion is browned, add the cooked beans and fry them well. Turn off the heat and get the masa dough, corn husks, and filling all lined up on the counter.

Wrapping a tamale prior to steaming.

The masa dough should be on the wet side, to make it more spreadable. Although most contemporary tamale recipes call for a generous amount of lard to be mixed with the masa dough. I feel this habit ruins the wonderful texture of the freshly made masa. In any case, putting lard in the masa dough was definitely not part of pre-Columbian tamale making.

Take enough wet masa dough to make a ball a little larger than a golf ball and spread it onto a corn husk until it covers the area of a small tortilla. It helps if the dough goes all the way into one corner of the husk. Put about one tablespoon of filling into the middle, and wrap the leaf around it tightly. The idea is to get the filling entirely surrounded by masa dough. The leaf can be tied with a thin piece of corn husk. If you're hosting a tamale party with multiple people wrapping, use the knots to differentiate the tamales—meat vs. vegetarian, etc.

Set the tamale into a steamer for cooking. You can steam in all kinds of things. Bamboo steamers work well, and many large pots these days come with steamer inserts. If you don't have a steamer, just put an old plate into a large pot with a small amount of water underneath it.

Steam for at least 40 minutes at a pretty good heat. I find they are easier to unwrap if they can cool for ten minutes after steaming. In any case they are too hot to eat right out of the steamer. Put your favorite hot sauce or salsa on, and enjoy one of the oldest recipes in the world.

Snacks

I'm a non-stop snacker! I detour through the kitchen as often as possible throughout the day. My philosophy on snacks has been to make them as healthy as possible. Yes, the snacks are going to involve some sugar, and some butter. But I try to sneak in as much good fiber and healthy flavor as possible. The following recipes reflect this instinct.

Kitchen Sink Cookies

Makes about 50 cookies

Butter	1 ½ cups
Dark brown sugar	1 cup
Honey or maple syrup	½ cup
Salt	1 teaspoon
Baking soda	½ teaspoon
Egg	1
Sourdough starter	½ cup
Corn meal	½ cup
Buckwheat flour	½ cup
Water	½ cup
Fresh rolled oats (or 1 cup, unrolled)	2 cups
Wheat flour	¾ cup
Dark chocolate chips	10 oz
Chopped nuts	1 cup

Cream the butter and sugar/honey with the vanilla first, then beat in the egg with the salt and baking soda. If you use unsalted butter you may need to add more than 1 teaspoon of salt. Buckwheat flour is a little strange to mix in so I recommend putting it in before the water. After the buckwheat flour is mixed in you can add the water and mix again. I add the ingredients in the order they appear in the list above.

Fresh rolled oats is an ingredient well worth pursuing. Any food store with a bulk section has a bin of whole oat "groats" these days, and they will stay fresh almost indefinitely. I don't grow oats yet, so for now I buy oats at the store. I have a three-roller counter top mill that is easy to use. The fresh taste of home-rolled oats is a significant departure from store-bought oats and I think it largely accounts for the raves I get for this cookie recipe. I typically measure out 1 cup of whole oats, prior to milling, for this recipe.

Milling the whole oats in oatmeal using the counter top three-roller mill.

Refrigerate the cookie dough overnight. This is a critical and necessary step to get the bran to soak up butter and moisture. The batter will be stiffer the next day. Getting the consistency right will be a matter of experimentation, since your grain and flour will be different from mine. Basically, you want the dough as wet as it can be without spreading out like a pancake on the cookie sheet.

Bake at 380 degrees for 8-9 minutes. I do not like what convection ovens do to these cookies, so I recommend regular baking on the middle or slightly above the middle oven rack. Remember that ovens vary in their actual temperature, so experiment and get the settings right for you. I also like to put the cookies onto a hot cookie sheet. Don't over bake them! That is a sin. I let the cookies cool and put them right back onto the cookie sheet and freeze them. A few hours later I put them into any handy plastic containers and store them in the freezer. Frozen chocolate chip cookies are the best!

Spritz Cookies

Makes about 50 cookies

Butter	1 cup
White sugar	2/3 cup
Egg	1
Salt	½ teaspoon
Almond extract	1 teaspoon
Flour	2 cups

I have been making spritz cookies since I was a small child. They are a classic butter cookie and the holidays don't seem complete without them. Making them with store-bought whole wheat flour would probably be a waste of good butter, but using fresh, high-extraction flour makes an outstanding holiday cookie.

Mix the butter, sugar, almond extract, and salt together first, then beat in the egg. Most people beat the stuffing out of it with a mixer, to create lightness. I have always just used a wooden spoon and never experienced someone turning down a cookie for lack of entrained air. Add the flour last and watch the consistency closely. Stiffen it up just enough so that the dough loses some of its stickiness. Usually when the dough pulls away from the sides of the bowl and forms an independent blob is the time to stop adding flour. Depending on how big your egg is, you may end up closer to 2⅓ cups of flour.

Use a cookie press to place the cookies onto a cold clean cookie sheet, sprinkle on some colored sugars, and bake them into a 400 degree oven for 6-8 minutes. You want to see basically one edge, of one cookie, on the sheet start to turn brown, then pull the cookies out.

The underside of the cookies should be just barely light brown. If the cookies stick to the sheet they are slightly undercooked, but probably OK. Overcooking is the greater evil.

Bread with Herb-Infused Olive Oil

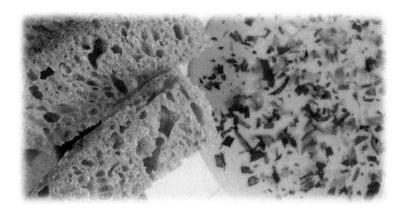

This recipe, technically an hors d'oeuvre, is guaranteed to get you invited back to any party you bring it along for. Don't tell anyone how easy it is.

Take your favorite dried herbs, crush them up, and put them in a pint mason jar that is half-filled with good olive oil. Oregano and rosemary, for starters, work fantastic. Put pepper flakes in if you like. Let the oil sit for a couple of days. When you're ready to use it, pour into a wide, shallow bowl and grate parmesan cheese on top. Now cut your bread into bite-sized pieces and start dipping.

Chips and Salsa

If you really want to go overboard with the "I made it myself" concept, consider making chips and salsa completely from scratch. Grow the corn, onions, tomatoes, peppers, and cilantro, and make everything up in your kitchen. If you want to "one-up" me, grow your own sunflowers and press them into oil. And dig your own salt mine.

Believe it or not, the effort will be worth it.

For the Chips

Tortillas	6
Oil	2-3 tablespoons

Start with making tortillas using the recipe on page 29. Coat the tortillas in oil, and cut into wedges. Fry them in a cast-iron frying pan for a few minutes, and finish in the oven at 350 degrees or so. They need to get completely dried out and crispy. Fifteen minutes total, turning after seven minutes, is about right.

For the Salsa

Tomatoes	1 lb
Yellow or white onion	medium
Garlic	a few cloves
Hot pepper	1 or 2
Cilantro	if you've got some
Salt	½ teaspoon or more

Snacks

Homemade salsa is never quite the same twice. I have the best luck with paste tomatoes, but I have messed with tomatillas and slicing tomatoes as well. The key to a fresh salsa is getting the texture right. The garlic and hot pepper should be evenly distributed, so they should be minced first. I've had good luck with both serrano and jalapeno peppers. Put everything into a food processor and give it all a quick chop. Make sure the salt is in there. Salsa is a bit like soup—it needs salt to bring out all the flavor.

I prefer to let the salsa sit for a few hours, or overnight, before using. The flavors seem to develop better.

Bread

Bread is the main driving force behind my work at Anarchy Acres. It was an interest in bread that first drove me to begin home-milling, and then home-growing and home-harvesting. Although I've added a lot of other interests, bread will always be my main passion here on the farm.

These are simple breads, largely free of nuts, honey, cinnamon, whatever. You can add these things to your bread if you like. My focus is on simple bread, made well. On the farm, I make primarily sourdough bread, which is the simplest possible leavened bread. From the first time I saw the ingredients on a package of sourdough bread in the store, I've been hooked. Flour, water, salt. Elegant simplicity. I eat about one loaf per week, year round. Here is how to make the bread I eat on Anarchy Acres.

Sourdough Starter

Weekly feeding

Water	¼ cup
Flour	½ cup

Sourdough starter is easy to take care of, especially when you use stone ground flour with plenty of bran and germ in it. Highly sifted flour, white flour, or nearly white flour, are more difficult to work with. Flour with the bran and germ removed do not support a healthy yeast colony as easily as whole flour does.

Feed your starter every week or two at the ratio of 2 parts flour to 1 part water, and keep it in a covered bowl or jar in the refrigerator. For most home bakers, a weekly feed of 1/4 water to 1/2 cup flour is perfect. Ideally, you'd like to feed the starter a day or two before using it in a recipe.

Excess starter can be used almost anywhere that you would use regular flour. Pancakes and cookies are two great places to put your extra starter. There is no reason to ever throw away your excess starter.

If your starter ever shows signs of mold, discard any trouble spots and feed normally. Similarly, if it dries out just dig some soft starter out of the middle and resume regular use. If you do completely lose your starter, just make a new one by mixing flour and water and feeding daily for a few days. It will reach full strength after a couple of weeks, but can be used in as little as two days.

2-1 Sourdough Bread

Makes 2 loaves (1 ½ pounds each)

This is the recipe I use for all the bread I regularly eat on the farm. Like any good sourdough bread, it will develop over the course of at least 24 hours, and often more. Don't worry, you won't actually be in the kitchen continuously for 24 or more hours! But bread is a matter of timing. Since I am a home chef, and I sleep at night, the bread cycle is based around a daily cycle.

After studying many bread recipes, I grew tired of the precise measuring and weighing of ingredients that nearly all bakers insist upon. To me, this custom lacks elegance. I eventually stumbled onto the realization that a 2:1 ratio of flour to water, by volume, is a very good seat-of-the-pants way to make a medium-high hydration dough. Everything in this recipe is 2:1. The starter gets fed 2:1, the levain is fed 2:1, and the final dough is fed 2:1. The final is also 2 times the levain.

High-hydration bread is a bit of a tightrope act. With added water comes great benefits— stretchy dough, big holes, and beautiful flavor. But it can be awkward to work with wet dough, and there is always a bit of drama when you try to get the dough to release from the rising basket. Don't hesitate to use more flour as you develop your bread making skills. And no matter what happens, the bread will taste great.`

Bake Day Minus 2: Feed the starter culture

Water	¼ cup
Flour	½ cup

Remove your starter from the fridge and feed it. Water for the starter, levain, and final should be approximately room termperature.

Bake Day Minus 1. Make the levain.

Sourdough starter	¼ cup
Flour	2 cups
Water	1 cups

Mix 1 cup of water with the starter, and mix in 2 cups of flour. Get the dough smooth, and put in a warm place for 4-8 hours. After the levain has puffed up and developed a few bubbles, it's time to make the final dough.

Final Dough

Flour	4 cups
Water	2 cups
Salt	1 tablespoon

Put two more cups of water with the dough and mix it in. Then add the flour and salt and do a rough mixing. You can do this with a wooden spoon or a dough hook on a mixer. But most of the work will be by hand.

I suggest the "slap and fold" technique for developing the dough. Plan on spending 20-30 minutes. The first five minutes will seem hopeless—the dough will be sticky and weak. But have faith and keep working the dough. Once it will hold shape, begin to slap and fold in earnest. Some sources recommend 600 slaps, but I doubt I ever get that far. Once the dough gets a smooth and shiny exterior, and your hands get mostly cleaned up, the dough is ready.

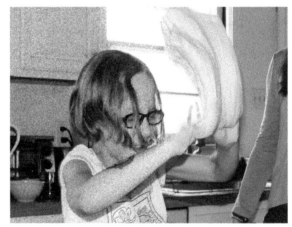
Slap and fold kneading is a great way to work with wet dough.

Alternative technique. Another way to deal with high-hydration dough is the "wet hand" technique. This will take more time, but require less physical effort. Put the dough in a bowl, wet your hands, and stretch it several times. Keep moving and stop before your hands get dry and the dough sticks. Do this every 20 minutes or so over the course of a couple hours.

Cover the dough and retard in the refrigerator for 12-24 hours.

Bake Day. I usually bake in the morning. Begin by removing the dough from the fridge and putting it in a warm place. Give the dough an hour or two and get the temperature above

55 degrees. You can put the bowl in a warm place or just dump the dough onto a counter, which will help draw out some of the cold.

Now get two rising forms ready. You can use a bowl with a floured kitchen towel, or a cane banneton. I use a mix of corn meal and flour to dust. Don't skimp on the dusting.

Divide the dough and begin shaping the first loaf. Use a rolling motion to continuously stretch the outside and push the developing membrane inward. You want to stretch the exterior as much as possible without tearing. Close up and pinch the area where you have been pushing the dough inward as much as possible. Now roll the nascent loaf in the mix of corn meal and flour and place into a banneton. Cover with a towel and let rise for an hour.

The dutch ovens should be intensively pre-heated to 450 degrees, or more if your oven allows. After one hour of rising, remove the hot dutch ovens and put them on the stove top. Working confidently, tip the contents of each banneton into your hand, and then into the dutch oven. Slash the top lightly with a wet, very sharp, kitchen knife. Put the cover on and get the whole thing back into your kitchen oven. I suggest investing in a reliable pair of oven mittens.

The loaf, ready to be covered and put into the oven for baking.

The loaves should be baked for 20 minutes with the covers on, and an additional 20 minutes with the cover off. If you pushed the temperature above 450 degrees, reduce it to exactly 450 for the last 20 minutes of the bake. Pull the loaves out when they are ready and cool on a rack.

I let my loaves cool completely before eating. I slice them up, put in a ziploc, and freeze the loaves. Most of the bread I eat comes out of the freezer in this manner.

No-Knead Bread

The philosophical opposite of artisan sourdough bread, no-knead bread is nevertheless healthy and great-tasting. I recommend it highly for people just starting out, or for those who are short on time. I believe that all bread bakers should try this recipe, to deepen one's understanding of fermentation and dough development. Here is my re-telling of the Jim Lahey/Mark Bittman classic.

Makes 1 loaf

Flour	3 cups
Instant yeast	¼ teaspoon
Salt	1 ¼ teaspoon
Water	1 ⅜ cup

I think of no-knead bread as a type of large, fermented pancake. It's almost impossible to screw up this bread, and the breezy, effortless nature of the recipe has been an inspiration to me and my baking.

Combine the dry ingredients in a bowl and then mix in the water. You will have an ugly, stringy dough without much body. Just mix it up with a wooden spoon, scrape the sides down, and cover for 12-18 hours at room temperature.

Using a generous coating of flour, dump the mass onto a counter and fold it a couple of times. You can use a dough knife or a spatula to help. Let the dough rest for 10-30 minutes, then form into a ball and place into a bowl lined with cloth that has been covered in flour. Now let the dough rise for around 2 hours.

Bread

At least 30 minutes before the dough is done rising, preheat the oven to 450 degrees and put an empty baking dish, with cover, into the oven to heat up. You can use a stoneware casserole dish, glass dish, or cast iron pot/dutch oven. Anything with a cover in the 4-8 quart range will work. When the dough is ready, remove the pot from the oven, dump the dough in, and put the cover on. You may want to shake the pot once or twice to get the dough to spread out. Bake in the oven for 40 minutes, and enjoy!

Dough for no-knead bread rising in a cloth-lined bowl.

Bread Machine Bread

Our heritage wheat flour works great in modern bread machines. You can find used bread machines at rummage sales and thrift stores, thus negating your last excuse for not making bread at home. Here is a recipe that works very well in my machine.

Makes 1 loaf (1 pound size)

Flour	2 cups
Active dry yeast	1 teaspoon
Salt	1 ¼ teaspoon
Water	¾ cup plus 1 tbsp.
Oil	1 ½ tablespoons
Honey	2 tablespoons
Dry milk powder	1 ½ tablespoons

This makes a healthy, great tasting back-to-school bread. Most bread machines have timers you can set to have warm bread when you wake up. Usually the bread takes about 4 1/2 hours on the "whole wheat" cycle, and it's a good idea to let it sit in the machine for another hour before removing it. So leave plenty of time if you use the overnight timer. Also, if you dig deeper into your bread machine recipe book you will find all kinds of variations with nuts, dried fruit etc.

Farm Pizza

Pizza, more than anything else, has driven my work with growing my own food and working with heritage grains. It's just such a fantastic reward. Pizza is also where a lot of things come together—grains, vegetables, and spices. Over the course of the year, I make many different pizzas with varying ingredients. What follows are some constants.

First, pizza is going to need some toppings. I always have basil pesto sauce on hand, as well as a tomato-based pizza sauce. Here's how I make these sauces.

Pesto Sauce

Fresh basil leaves	3 cups
Fresh parsley leaves	½ cup
Garlic	3 or more cloves
Parmesan or asiano cheese, grated	1 cup
Pine nuts	½ cup
Olive oil	¼ cup
Salt	to taste
Pepper and additional spices	optional

I rarely have any good parsley around, so my pesto is usually just basil. The hardest part is picking the leaves and washing them. If you take the time to carefully pluck each leaf and discard any hint of a stem, the result will be sweeter. Stems are bitter. It's a big help to have a salad spinner for the washing process.

Once the leaves are washed and dried, pesto is a cakewalk. Put all the ingredients into a decent food processor and let loose. It won't take long to mix everything and get the pesto formed. You can vary the olive oil content to get the consistency you like. Pesto should be used or frozen right away. Small plastic containers work great, but you can also fill up ice cube trays with pesto and then put the frozen cubes into a plastic bag.

Pizza Sauce

Tomatoes	enough to fill up your big pot, 10 lbs or so
Onion	1 or 2
Garlic	plenty
Herbs	yes
Salt and pepper	to taste

I have the best luck with paste tomatoes—Amish Paste, Roma, San Marzano, etc. Although I've made good pizza sauce with Purple Cherokee tomatoes, I now use only paste tomatoes if I can.

It's well worth the time to get the skins off. Start a big pot of boiling water on the stove, and put small batches of tomatoes in for 30 seconds or so. This scalds the skins and it's then easy to pull off most of the skin with your fingers. Clean it up with a knife and dump into another big pot. Once the pot is full of skinned tomatoes, put it on the stove on low and start simmering your tomatoes. This will be a couple hours. The degree to which you reduce the sauce is a matter of personal taste, but it should be reduced by at least two-thirds to make a sauce that will stick.

I like to run my sauce through a hand-cranked ricer at some point. This helps break down any fibers in the tomatoes and strains off some of the seeds. If the tomatoes are small, they can go right into the ricer after being skinned. I've also done this step after simmering for an hour or so.

After the sauce has thickened for a couple of hours, I fire up a cast-iron skillet and fry up some chopped onions. The onions get stirred into the sauce, and it's now time to add garlic and other spices, too. I use a garlic crusher to add at least six large garlic cloves, and I also grind in plenty of black pepper, too. Salt is a requirement for any vegetable sauce, so put enough in so the flavor comes out. I also put in at least two basil pesto ice cubes, but you don't have to.

Although you can scald some mason jars and can the sauce as you would tomatoes, I always freeze my pizza sauce. Plastic containers of almost any size will work great. You will thaw out the containers on "pizza day," use as much sauce as you need, and simply put the unused sauce back into the freezer. Easy and quick.

Farm Pizza

Pizza Dough

You can use almost any sourdough or yeast bread dough to make pizza crust dough. I use the 2-1 Sourdough recipe on page 59, adding 1 cup extra of flour in the final dough to stiffen it up a bit. The No-Knead bread recipe on page 62 can also be used to make a good pizza dough, again just by adding flour, about ½ cup in this case.

Here's one more option for pizza dough, in this case, a traditional yeast pizza dough.

Overnight Pizza Dough

Flour	3 cups
Honey or sugar	2 tablespoons
Salt	1 ½ teaspoons
Water	1 ⅓ cups
Olive oil	1 tablespoon

In a large bowl, mix flour, salt, and yeast. In a separate bowl, whisk together water, oil, and honey. Add to the flour mixture and mix until a soft dough forms. It will be stickier than typical bread or pizza dough. Now cover the bowl with plastic wrap or a moist towel and refrigerate for at least 24 hours. It can stay in the fridge for multiple days if needed. Just pull it out and let it warm up a bit before using. Makes 2 large pizzas or 4-6 personal size pizzas, depending on how thin you roll the crust.

Baking Options

You're going to have to bake these pizzas somewhere. I use two options on the farm. The first is my wood-fired brick oven. This is the gold standard, and I don't know any type of oven that does a better job. The oven is out on the back patio, and it works very well for bread and pizza. It also has the capacity to make a lot of pizzas if I host a gathering. My record for the wood-fired oven is about 50 pizzas in 2 hours!

Unfortunately, a wood-fired oven take about three to four hours to heat up and needs a lot of tending. It's also outside, and it gets cold in Wisconsin. So I also make a lot of pizza in my ordinary gas range. I have a set of firebricks that will completely line one of the racks, making a passable pizza deck. If you want to do this, get the "half-thick" firebricks, which are about 1¼ inches thick. Full thickness bricks will be too heavy for most oven racks. You can also use a pizza stone indoors, but the firebricks will give you much more thermal mass. If you do use your indoor oven, get it absolutely as hot as you can. Six hundred degrees would be best, but I don't know any home ovens that get that hot. You'll have to settle for around 475 degrees.

There is a third option in between these two systems. A pizza stone or firebricks can be placed onto a charcoal grill. This means you'll be cooking outdoors, but the charcoal grill can get hotter than your indoor oven. A hot oven will result in a lighter, crispier crust.

Time to Make Pizza (For Four Pizzas)

Pizza dough	2 pounds
Basil pesto or pizza sauce	2 cups
Chopped spinach	optional
Cheese, grated or sliced	1 pound
Pepperoni or sausage	optional
Garlic scapes, chopped	optional
Basil leaves	if in season
Sliced or chopped sweet peppers	2 cups
Dried herbs and spices	to taste
Salt and black pepper	yes

Divide the dough and roll into tight balls. Dust with flour and leave covered on the counter until you are ready to roll out the dough. This is bread dough, and although it doesn't have to rise, it helps the texture if it's given time to develop. An hour at 72 degrees is perfect.

To form the crust, set up on the counter with a rolling pin and flour for dusting. Press the dough into a circle with your hands as much as possible, then finish with the rolling pin. Turn and dust often. If the crust loses its round shape, use the roller to push dough where it's needed.

Pizza on a corn-meal dusted peel, ready to slide into a hot oven.

Gently transfer the rolled-out dough to a wooden pizza peel with a generous coating of corn meal. Use your fingers to finish shaping and stretching the crust. We're ready for toppings!

Beginners tend to put too many toppings on, so start out sparingly. The sauce goes on first (pesto, tomato, or both), followed by any green leafy toppings. Chopped spinach is just heavenly, and basil leaves work very well also. Now sprinkle the cheese on, using less than you think is needed. Finish with peppers and any meat you want. I love to put minced garlic scapes on as well, but I can't get many followers for this concept. I suspect I've lived on a farm too long now, and just can't judge when I've gone overboard with garlic.

Black pepper, herbs, and salt go last. If you've made the sauce from scratch, be aware of the need for salt. Even really high quality ingredients lose their flavor in a zero-salt environment. Use enough to bring out the flavor.

Pizza baking in a wood-fired brick oven--the gold standard!

Before sliding the pizza into your chosen oven, wiggle the peel and make sure the dough will slide off easily. If the dough sticks, carefully loosen it up with a knife, and use more corn meal next time. With one motion, slide the pizza into the oven, and pay close attention. If you're lucky enough to bake in a really hot oven, the pizzas will cook in as little as 45 seconds. Wood-fired ovens tend to have hot spots, so be prepared to pull the pizza out and spin it a bit to help even out the cooking.

Indoors, you're probably looking at a 6-8 minute cook time, or more. Let the crust and the cheese bubble up well before pulling out and eating. Dig right in—it's a sin to let pizza get cold!

I nearly always bake more pizzas than I can eat, so I can put some in the freezer. Let the pizzas cool on a rack, then put in the freezer on something that will keep them flat. When all the pizzas are well-frozen, you can stack them in a big plastic bag. For reheating, I suggest 425 degrees on the center rack, without a pizza stone or firebricks. The crust will crisp up nicely, and the pizza should be ready to eat after 10-12 minutes.

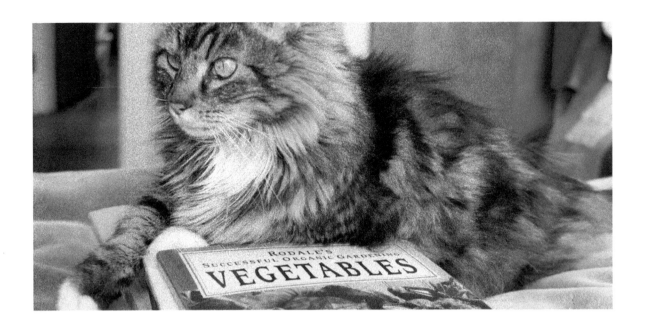

Resources

If you've made it this far, you're a believer in books and resources. The more knowledge you have, the better decisions you can make in the field and in the kitchen. Here are some books and resources that have inspired me in my cooking, and my lifestyle.

From Aspargus to Zucchini: A Guide to Farm-Fresh Seasonal Produce. Madison Area Community Supported Agriculture Coalition, 2003. This comprehensive guide to common farm produce contains quick tips for storage and cooking, and a few recipes for each vegetable. Keep a copy handy in your kitchen.

The Bread Book: A Natural, Whole-Grain Seed-to-Loaf Approach to Real Bread. Thom Leonard, 1990. This book describes how to grow wheat in your own back yard, harvest the grain, mill into flour, and make bread at home. There is even a good how-to section for making your own backyard brick oven.

Rodale's Successful Organic Gardening Vegetables. Patricia S. Michalak, 1993. Excellent A-Z index of common vegetables, with planting dates, growing guidelines, and harvesting information. A great reference for keeping your crops managed throughout the season.

Five Acres and Independence: A Handbook for Small Farm Management. M.G. Kains, 1940. Although this classic from the mid-20th Century lacks concern about fertilizer or fossil fuel inputs, the spirit is still well within my ideal.

Resources

Weed the Soil, Not the Crop: A Whole Farm Approach to Weed Management. Anne and Eric Nordell, 2009. A very creative and simple strategy for rotating crops on the small, animal-powered farm.

Crop Rotation and Cover Cropping: Soil Resiliency and Health on the Organic Farm. Seth Kroeck, 2004. Understanding crop rotation is key to successfully growing crops year after year without outside chemical inputs.

The New Horse-Powered Farm: Tools and Systems for the Small-Scale Sustainable Market Gardener. Stephen Leslie, 2013. Excellent overview of modern animal-powered farming and instructions for almost every aspect of market gardening with little or no fossil fuel energy.

The Woodright's Shop: A Practical Guide to Traditional Woodcraft. Roy Underhill, 1981. A good overview of basic woodworking skills that come in very handy on the small homestead.

Wheat Growing in Wisconsin. Edmond Joseph Delwiche, B. D. Leith, 1919. Published by the forerunner of the University of Wisconsin Agricultural Extension, this farmer's pamphlet has been the inspiration behind my efforts to seek out and revive the wheat of nineteenth-century Wisconsin.

A Sand County Almanac: And Sketches Here and There. Aldo Leopold, 1949. Beautiful essays about the changing seasons, written by the legendary UW biology professor. "A thing is right when it tends to preserve the integrity, stability, and beauty of the biotic community. It is wrong when it tends otherwise."

Foxfire Books. Eliot Wigginton, 1967–. For over 40 years, high school students in Foxfire programs have helped to gather and publish information about their Southern Appalachian heritage. Self-reliance and traditional skills are highlighted throughout in an interview-style format.

The Joy of Living: Unlocking the Secret and Science of Happiness. Eric Swanson and Yongey Mingyur Rinpoche, 2007. Learn to meditate while weeding!

Rural Heritage Magazine. RuralHeritage.com. This excellent periodical will connect you with the animal-powered agricultural community.

Small Farmer's Journal. SmallFarmersJournal.com. Quarterly publication devoted to small-scale organic farming.

Anarchy Acres Website. AnarchyAcres.com. Our online presence for selling fresh-milled flour from the Wisconsin heritage wheat we grow. Use the "Contact Us" page to send me any questions or comments you have about the recipes in this book.

About the Author

    Wisconsin native Charlie Tennessen lives in Mount Pleasant, WI, on his four-acre farm known as Anarchy Acres. Three donkeys, two sheep, three goats, a dozen chickens, and several cats all share their lives with Charlie on this remarkable farm.

Index

Index

anarchy
acres

CPSIA information can be obtained
at www.ICGtesting.com
Printed in the USA
FSHW02n0837110518
47855FS